Hazel King

# THE CLOTHING INDUSTRY

REVISED AND UPDATED

Trends in Textile Technology

Heinemann
LIBRARY

**www.heinemann.co.uk/library**
Visit our website to find out more information about Heinemann Library books.

To order:
☎ Phone 44 (0) 1865 888066
▤ Send a fax to 44 (0)1865 314091
▨ Visit the Heinemann Library Bookshop at www.heinemann.co.uk/library to browse our catalogue and order online.

First published in Great Britain by Heinemann Library, Halley Court, Jordan Hill, Oxford OX2 8EJ, part of Harcourt Education.
Heinemann Library is a registered trademark of Harcourt Education Ltd.

Editorial: Sarah Shannon
Design: Philippa Jenkins
Picture Research: Hannah Taylor
Production: Duncan Gilbert

Originated by Chroma Graphics
Printed and bound in China by Leo Paper Group

ISBN 978 0 431 99014 9
12 11 10 09 08
10 9 8 7 6 5 4 3 2 1

**British Library Cataloguing in Publication Data**
King, Hazel
    The clothing industry. - 2ed.
    - (Trends in textile technology)
    1.Clothing trade - Juvenile literature
    338.4'7687
A full catalogue record for this book is available from the British Library.

**Acknowledgements**
The publishers would like to thank the following for permission to reproduce photographs: ©Alamy Images p. 5 (Nick Hanna); ©Corbis pp. 19 (Jacqui Hurst), 21 (Bettmann); ©Eye Ubiquitous pp. 7 (sportshoot), 22 (Steve Lindridge), 27 (Bennett Dean); ©Gerber Technology p.25; ©Harcourt Education Ltd./Gareth Boden pp.9, 10, 20, 23, 26; ©Image Bank p.6 (Darren Clark); ©Rex Features pp.14 (Sipa Press), 16 (Steve Wood); ©Stock Market pp.4 (Chuck Savage), 28 (William Taufic), 38 (John Henley); ©Tony Stone Images pp.8 (Bruce Ayres), 29 (Lori Adamski Peek), 30 (Paul Redman), 31 (Bob Thomas), 32 (Chris Shinn), 40 (Timothy Shonnard), 42 (Roger Tully), 43 (Steve Weinberg); ©Trip pp.12 (H Rogers), 17 (A Cowin).

Cover photograph of shirts hanging on a rail reproduced with permission of Corbis/Imagemore Co. Ltd.

Our thanks to Carey Clarkson for her assistance during the preparation of this book.

Every effort has been made to contact copyright holders of any material reproduced in this book. Any omissions will be rectified in subsequent printings if notice is given to the publishers.

Any words appearing in the text in bold, **like this**, are explained in the Glossary.

# Contents

# The business of clothes

The British clothing industry not only produces a wide variety of **outputs** – clothes of all shapes and sizes for all ages – but also involves a wide range of company types. The significance of clothing manufacture in British industry is likely to remain for some time to come. Like many areas of manufacture, it has had to face change in recent years. This has been as much a result of change in the fashion world as technological advances.

Clothing manufacturers may be very small scale, producing a low volume for a limited **market** and employing only the minimum of staff. At the other extreme, companies may have a huge output with a large market, and employ thousands of workers.

## Street fashion

There is a more relaxed and varied approach to fashion now. People are choosing clothes they feel comfortable in rather than those that are regarded as 'fashionable'. British society is no longer prepared to have its hemline dictated by designers. Street fashion is a strong feature of today's clothing industry.

Street fashion can be seen in most high street stores. It is an example of affordable fashion for the mass population, marketed at young people likely to want something new in a few weeks' time. The clothes are not meant to have a particularly long life, so their price tag is usually moderate. Street fashion has been made possible by the wider range of cheaper fabrics and faster production methods due to technological advances.

## Staple garments

In contrast to the fast turnover of street fashions, another sector of the clothing market manufactures staple garments. These are clothes that are not greatly influenced by fashion and include schoolwear, shirts and underwear. Consumers demand staple garments regularly and in large numbers. It is not uncommon for an adult to own 20 pairs of briefs whereas in the 1940s or 1950s, 3 or 4 pairs would have been acceptable. Companies producing staple garments can set their production processes to run for months, or even years, without a great deal of alteration in style.

Your coursework task may ask you to consider various retail outlets as a specific user for your textile product. Knowing where you will market your item(s) can help you to identify useful points for your design specification. You will need to know what the different retail environments aim to provide and what the advantages and disadvantages of each of these are.

Street fashion is affordable fashion marketed mainly at young people.

Market stalls are great places for picking up a bargain.

# Types of retailer

**Independents** – are retailers with fewer than 10 outlets. Most are sole traders with only one shop or boutique. They offer a personal touch and often specialize in a certain style of textile product. Higher running costs mean products can be are more expensive. They have less **stock** and are more cautious when buying or marking down stock items.

**Multiples** – are chains of shops owned by a large company e.g. Gap. They can afford prime sites and generate a high turnover. They buy in bulk and have extensive ranges. Consumers can expect to find moderate fashion at a mid-price point in 'multiple' stores.

**Department Stores** – offer a wide variety of goods (around 70% being fashion) in different departments and are designed to keep the consumer in the store for as long as possible. They offer incentives such as concession trading, loyalty cards and target specific groups with promotional material.

**Concessions** – take the risk out of retail. The department store lets out space to a retailer or manufacturer for a fixed rate. This provides for a more diverse range of products and is a useful way for young designers to get their foot on the ladder. Testing the market without the risk and high costs attached to a shop.

**Discounters** – buy stock at reduced rates from a variety of sources. They have a 15% share of the market as they offer competitive prices. They often remove labels so the consumer cannot identify the manufacturer.

**Factory shops** – developed from the overstocks and faulty goods produced by manufacturers.

Originally these were offered to employees, but over time, manufacturers have opened their doors to the wider public. Factory shops are often in out-of-town shopping parks and offer high quality and competitive prices.

**Markets** – can usually be depended on for a bargain! The items sold tend to be from similar sources as those used by discounters. Damaged or rejected products often called 'seconds' are offered cheaply to market traders. Specialist markets can offer a wealth of inspiration and lovely antique fabrics and attract young designers and students as a cheaper way to test market preferences.

**Mail order** – suits the consumer who cannot, or does not want to, go shopping. 'Magalogues' are now the new style of catalogue and take the form of a monthly magazine.

**Electronic shopping** – is a development of mail order made possible by changing technologies and fashion websites. Home shopping through interactive TV is also growing in popularity. The main advantage is that the facility is open 24 hours and opens up the market to the consumer abroad. Fashion advertising and shopping websites are a great research source for coursework tasks.

# Clothes and the consumer

## Consumer satisfaction

The main aim of the clothing industry is to provide garments that consumers want to buy. A garment must satisfy all of a consumer's needs. When someone looks at a garment in a shop, they often focus first on the colour, fabric design and shape of the garment. Together, these aspects provide an immediate visual image. They are the basis for whether or not the garment is appealing. If it does appeal, trying it on may be the next step, and then other considerations come into play – for example, how well it fits, how comfortable it is, when and where it can be worn, what it goes with, its brand name, how it can be washed and, of course, its price.

Naturally the considerations which are most important will depend on the type of garment and on the individual consumer. If someone is happy with the garment and purchases it, the manufacturer has successfully satisfied the consumer's needs.

When browsing in a clothes shop you are likely to focus on the colour, fabric design and shape of the garment.

## Retailer satisfaction

The clothing industry cannot survive just by pleasing its customers. It must also make a profit. This is essential as without a profit a business cannot survive. As long as the consumer is content that the product they have bought is good value for money, then everyone involved in making, selling and buying is content. This success is largely dependent on good **marketing**. Marketing is the way a manufacturer or retailer **promotes** their product. There are a variety of ways of marketing, including the use of advertising, effective packaging and display of goods.

## Marketing department

Large clothing manufacturers will have a marketing department, or a company will employ a manager who is responsible for the marketing of the clothes produced. The marketing manager or department has three main areas of responsibility: marketing, merchandising and sales.

### Marketing

One aspect of marketing is **market research**, which aims to establish **perceived consumer need**, that is to find out what consumers want and need. Market research can help to identify a gap in the market. This occurs when consumers want, but currently cannot buy, a particular item. When marketing reveals a gap or 'niche', this is known as niche marketing. As long as there is sufficient demand and it is possible to make the item at a profit, then a manufacturer can fill the gap or niche.

As well as identifying gaps in the market, marketing also promotes existing goods.

Athletes can publicize a company's name and logo.

This is so that consumers are aware of the products already on sale.

Clothing manufacturers rely on their marketing department to select the relevant research methods needed to find out where there is a niche in the market. Similarly, you need to be able to select the correct methods of research to help you to find out what products already exist on the market and what your target group needs.

## Research styles

Retailers will work out the profile of their target customers by:

- Observing and counting who comes through the door.
- Tracking popular items - an electronic point-of-sale (EPOS) device tracks items that sell well and re-orders stock.
- Analysing national census data to show shop retail performance, broad trends and economic conditions.

This is not very different from how research could be completed for coursework:

- Consumer survey/questionnaire to build up a customer profile.
- Use of the internet and CD-Roms – remember to analyse your findings not just print it out!
- Product analysis – looking at an existing product in relation to your target group.
- Charting market products – looking at a range of relevant existing products.
- Mood Board – keep it relevant and make sure to annotate your ideas and findings in relation to the design brief and the target group.

## Promoting goods

All sales promotion, whether aimed at the public or retailers, is based on effective communication. Communication is important because it can establish a company's name and image, which should lead to increased sales. Promotion can be carried out through:

- advertising in newspapers, magazines, radio, television and the Internet
- publicity from other people – e.g. when famous people wear particular clothes, perhaps with a logo or designer label
- personal selling is likely to occur when manufacturers are demonstrating their latest range to potential **clients** (retailers)
- presentations such as fashion shows are probably the most visual and effective way to promote clothes; they are held regularly by designers and manufacturers but retailers occasionally put on fashion shows for their customers.

# A design process

## Garment designers

As well as receiving advice from retailers, the garment designers must themselves stay on top of fashion trends. They also need to know the manufacturer's production requirements and what the manufacturing plant is capable of producing. This way they can offer designs that can be realistically produced and satisfy the perceived consumer need.

This process is not as easy as it sounds. Change happens quickly in fashion, and design ideas are constantly being proposed, discussed and modified. A contract for a series of garments cannot be confirmed until the type, colour and design of fabric, trimmings, silhouette and cost have all been decided. Even after all this, the garments continue to be developed as the technical aspects of fit, **grading**, construction and **garment performance** are considered.

## Design process

The process of garment design can be divided into four stages.

1 Design initiation – the first stage is to assess consumer needs and use them to determine colour, silhouette, style and fabric design.
2 Design concept – at this stage many design options are explored. Designs that satisfy perceived consumer needs are produced as design offers.
3 Decision-making process – design offers are considered and used to develop a range of designs. Decisions are made about the choice of designs, fabric, trimmings etc.
4 Technical design – finally, the design offer that has been accepted must be refined so that it precisely fulfills the fit, construction, garment performance and production requirements.

A garment designer will modify a garment during the design process.

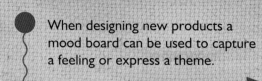

When designing new products a mood board can be used to capture a feeling or express a theme.

# Design research

There are various types of research that need to be carried out during the process of designing and making garments. Initially, market research is needed to find out what consumers like and don't like. Designers carry out research to help them with their ideas. They often develop a **mood board**, which will involve researching colour schemes, fabric types, images, consumer preferences and so on. Once sufficient research has been carried out, designers can begin to sketch their ideas and perhaps make a **prototype**.

A prototype is a model of an idea. It is made to see how well the idea works. In clothes design a prototype is important to ensure the pattern pieces fit together correctly and the garment has the right look or image. Prototypes of garments are often referred to as **toiles**. Toiles are usually made out of calico or a similar, cheap fabric. Initially, a toile might be put on a mannequin, which is a wooden or plastic human dummy. The mannequin's size can be altered slightly but a model (or the **client**) would need to try on the toile to ensure an exact fit.

You need to make a prototype of a pattern as well, particularly if the design is complex. The pattern pieces are pinned or stuck to represent the way the item will be joined. Although paper does not hang in the same way as fabric, it is more economical to test and alter a paper pattern than to find you need to make alterations after the fabric has been cut.

# Sample clothes

The prototype pattern is used to make a sample garment. This process is carried out by a skilled machinist, who works out how best to join the pieces together. After the sample garments are completed and the production process has been established, the production costs can be predicted. Quality and performance checks are then carried out on the garments, and pattern pieces are produced. These are used for the grading and **marker planning** processes.

Finally, a **product specification** can be written. This contains precise details about the garment so that it can be reproduced on a large scale.

# Clothing manufacture

No matter how large or small a clothing manufacturer, the production process will involve more or less the same stages:

1 Cutting – this includes a variety of procedures being carried out in order to turn fabrics and other **components** into cut garments.

2 Sewing – this is when garments are assembled. Cut garments are sewn and under-pressed and quality checks take place. Other operations such as embroidery or pleating may be done at this stage or they may be completed by an **outside contractor**.

3 Pressing – the final or top pressing takes place.

4 Finishing – the stage at which labels and tags for hanging a garment are attached.

5 Final inspection – when garments, or a selection of them, are inspected before being packaged.

6 Packing – the final stage, when garments are either hung or folded and then bagged or boxed, depending on the type of garment and retail outlet.

Highly fashionable items have a short life span.

## Fabric selection

Selecting the correct fabric for your design is crucial to the overall success of your garment. Manufacturers and designers have various fabric outlets that they visit to gain ideas about current trends and costs, before finally selecting the fabrics for their collection. Fabric fairs and trade shows are popular market places to promote and forecast new ideas in fabrics.

When selecting a fabric you need to consider the visual and technical properties of a fabric alongside its feel or handle. The characteristics of a fibre, its weight, warmth, appearance, and the way it behaves, determine the qualities and purposes for which woven and knitted fabrics are made or used. Fabrics are constructed to be touched and there is no substitute for feeling a fabric to assess its drape, surface characteristics and weight. When choosing a suitable fabric consider the following points:

- Check the selvedge to see if the fabric is straight.
- Knit and woollen fabrics are liable to pilling. Rub the surface of the fabric to see if fibres come off.
- Check printed fabrics for an even print, look to see if the scale of the print looks right against the body.
- Check for weaving or dyeing irregularities.
- Move to a natural light source to assess the colour at its most natural.

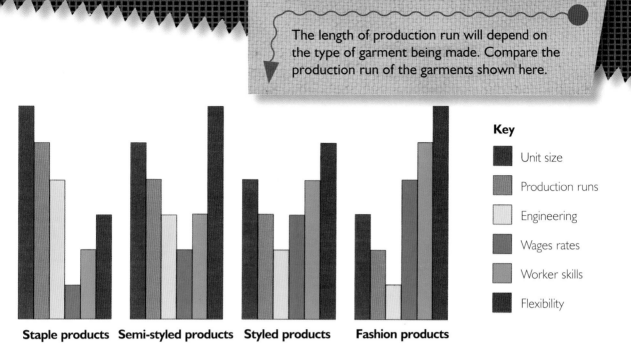

**Key**

- ■ Unit size
- ■ Production runs
- □ Engineering
- ■ Wages rates
- ■ Worker skills
- ■ Flexibility

**Staple products    Semi-styled products    Styled products    Fashion products**

- Check fabric recovery by squeezing a piece of the fabric in your hand a few times and assessing the stretch rate.
- Fold or drape the fabric to see how it hangs.
- Check to assess fraying qualities. Tease the threads to see if it will pull apart easily.
- Check the handle of the fabric – feel the surface and assess its warmth, coolness, dryness, how slippery it is etc.

## Types of production

Not all types of manufacture are suitable for all types of garment. A production run is the length of time for which one garment type will be produced. The length of the production run will have an effect on all other aspects of manufacture, such as the size of the factory or unit.

The length of production run depends on the type of garment being made:

- Staple garments – these are produced continuously and only require minor changes in colour, cut and fabric, so their manufacture is relatively straightforward. Examples include underwear and workclothes such as overalls.
- Semi-styled products – garments that are also mass produced but require more frequent changes in style, such as men's shirts. The fabric and style may alter quite frequently so production runs are shorter than staple garments.
- Clothes that frequently alter in style include women's skirts and dresses. These are styled products and production runs have to be short to allow for considerable changes in fabric, colour and design.
- Highly fashionable items have a short lifespan. They are produced very quickly and in very short runs. Each style may be totally unique in shape, colour and design. These are known as fashion products.

The bar charts above show how different types of garment production affect other aspects of manufacturing.

# Commercial Production

The three types of production are job production, batch production and mass or flow production.

Mass production is defined as the manufacture of goods in large quantities, often using standardized designs and assembly-line techniques. Modern mass-production methods have led to improvements in the cost, quality, quantity, and variety of goods available on the market today. The requirements for mass production of a particular product are based on the existence of a consumer market large enough to justify a large investment.

Batch production is defined as the process where products are produced in batches and where each separate batch consists of a number of the same products.

Batch production is a popular method to deal with ready-to-wear (RTW) designer label textile items, eg Designers at Debenhams. Garments are designed to fit a range of standard sizes and shapes and patterns are developed from a basic block using CAD.

A sample garment is made up in a medium size, from the intended fabric. Once the design has been approved it is put into production in a range of standard sizes. They are sold through up-market retailers.

This method of production involves a high-level of design, pattern making and sampling skills. The benefits of this system is the use of cost-effective materials and lower manufacturing costs.

## Just in Time (JIT)

This system is developed to ensure that raw materials and components arrive as they are needed. This system saves the company time and money in tied up stock and storage space. Retailers like 'Top Shop' and 'Zara' use JIT to enable them to change their fashion lines quickly to keep up with consumer trends.

Manufacturers use JIT systems to reduce the amount of stock held, reducing costs and producing shorter runs of one product in different fabrics. This system requires constant communication with suppliers to ensure reliable delivery of last minute orders.

Precision Stitching Ltd. manufactures and supplies Bean Bags. The company uses CAD and CAM technology in the design and production of all their products, ensuring that both quality and precision are included in the manufacturing process. Due to this, the 'Quality Guarantee' provided by greatbeanbags.com has become the industry standard. Alongside the

An example of a 'stand-up' assembly system.

CAD/CAM technology in design and production the company also has branding facilities such as embroidery, with full embroidery disc design and generation at their factory in Nottingham.

## Off the peg manufacture

This refers to textile products which are cheaper as they are made to fit standard average sizes. When producing off the peg garments the standard template can be used for the whole production run. This allows a batch of items to be made at one time keeping costs low and making items less expensive.

## Assembly line production.

This is an industrial arrangement of machines, equipment, and workers for a continuous flow of work pieces in mass-production operations. An assembly line is designed by looking at the process of manufacture of each component as well as the final product. The movement of material is made as simple and short as possible, with no cross flow or backtracking. Work assignments, numbers of machines, and production rates are planned so that all the operations performed along the assembly line are compatible.

Automated assembly lines consist entirely of machines and are used in such industries as petroleum refining and chemical manufacture and in many modern automobile-engine plants.

## Division of labour systems

Division of labour means that a job is divided into a number of steps, and then groups of workers are employed to carry out each step. Each group specializes in a specific part of the garment construction. Doing the job in a routine way, produces more than if each worker had to carry out all the stages of manufacture. However, the system has been criticized for neglecting the skills of workers and removing their involvement with the end product. This type of production can also be referred to as section system or cell production.

## New thoughts, old traditions

The clothing industry traditionally consisted of production workers who performed the cutting and sewing functions in an assembly line. The industry today, remains labour-intensive, despite advances in technology and workplace practices. Production work is increasingly contracted out to foreign suppliers to take advantage of lower labour costs abroad. A growing number of clothing manufacturers are performing only the entrepreneurial functions involved such as buying raw materials, designing clothes and accessories, preparing samples, arranging for production and distribution, and marketing the finished product.

In industry today many production workers work in teams. For example, sewing machine operators are organized into production "modules." Each operator is trained in the functions required to assemble a garment. Each module is responsible for its own performance, and individuals usually receive compensation based on the team's performance.

The textile and clothing industries are rapidly modernizing with advanced machinery boosting productivity levels. Computers and computer-controlled equipment are now used to perform many functions. Wider looms and the increasing use of robotics make production more efficient. Despite these changes, the clothing industry has remained significantly less automated than many other manufacturing industries.

# Clothing technology

There are many different systems used in the clothing industry to produce garments or outputs. The type of approach used by a manufacturer will depend on the nature of the clothes and the size of the organization. A production system may be totally manual, where everything is done by hand, or totally automated, where everything is done by machine. However, most systems use a combination of these methods.

## 'Making through'

'Making through' is a traditional method of clothing manufacture. In this system a garment is made from start to finish by the same person. The operator is given a bundle of cut items which he or she then assembles using hand and machine stitching. The operator must be highly skilled as well as versatile. This is a **labour-intensive** method of manufacture and therefore the clothes are expensive. However, it is regarded as the most rewarding of the systems of manufacture as it is less repetitive for the worker and gives them a sense of ownership of the final garment. Today, **bespoke** clothing might use the making through production method.

## Section system

When making clothes using the section system, operators specialize in the assembly of one part of a garment. They do all the tasks required to complete that section or component of the finished article.

## Progressive bundles

In the progressive bundle system of manufacture, clothes are assembled gradually.

Bespoke tailoring is an example of the 'making through' production method.

As the name implies, they are put together as they progress through the system. Each section of work has a store at either side so completed work from the previous stage can be stored ready for one set of operators while their work is stored for the next series of operators. This system is versatile and efficient and is used for large-scale production.

## Straight line system

The straight line system is also used when large quantities of clothing are being manufactured. Tasks are organized according to the time they take to complete rather than the order in which the garments are put together. This means the success of the system is based on efficient timing.

## Conveyor belts

Conveyor belts have been used for many years in the clothing industry to transport garments, or parts of garments, from operator to operator. However, today's computerized systems of feeding and controlling production have led to a faster and more efficient industry. Operators are positioned at work stations and the selective conveyor belt system automatically feeds the operator with work and takes completed items to the next stage or operator.

## UPS

The UPS (unit production system) uses computers to plan, control and direct the flow of work through a system. A unit of production is a whole garment (rather than a bundle) which is automatically taken from work station to work station. The flow of production has already been decided and the computer is set accordingly. Each garment component is brought as close to the operator as possible. This reduces the amount of movement required by the operator to grab and position the next item to be stitched. This type of computerized system is likely to be found in the mass production of clothes. It is expensive but it has the advantage of being able to respond quickly to changes in fashion.

## Quick response

The quick response sewing system was first developed in Japan. It is important because it allows manufacturing adjustments to be made quickly as the market changes. Each work station has two to four machines and one operator takes a garment through the necessary tasks, including pressing, before it is passed on to the next work station. All the components of a garment are loaded on to a hanging clamp attached to a trolley. This is then transported by a computer-controlled overhead trolley system, rather than a conveyor belt. Each work station is kept informed about the style of garment being worked on via the computerized trolley.

The GERBERmover GM-300 is a fully computerized unit production system. It uses an overhead conveyor to transport products from work station to work station, one product at a time. Operations can even be performed without removing parts from the hanger.

# One-off production

When products are made specifically for a consumer or client, the production method is known as one-off production. This means one garment or outfit has been made to suit and fit that person; it would be a unique accessory. Equally, a consumer can choose a garment from a range in a shop and then have that garment made-to-measure. Although someone else may have the same style of clothing, the consumer has one that has been made to fit perfectly.

## Bespoke tailoring

This is the name given to the production of custom-made clothes. Traditionally all clothes were made by hand for individual customers because there was no such thing as mass production. Today suits are often made this way, particularly for men. As the suit is still the traditional outfit for many jobs, it is important that they fit well and are comfortable. The customer chooses a particular style of suit and the type of fabric. Measurements are taken and during production the customer will have a fitting so the tailor can make any necessary adjustments. Such custom-made clothes are expensive because production is time-consuming and labour-intensive.

## Haute couture

As a method of production, **haute couture** is time-consuming, expensive and labour-intensive. It requires a high level of skill from everyone involved in the garment's manufacture. It is thought that there are only about 2000 women in the world who can afford haute couture. Yet, it continues to exist as an exclusive sector of the clothing industry.

An example of haute couture.

## One-off production

This method of production is the designing and making of a single textile product to a client's specification. The garment design is developed from a basic pattern, with a prototype made from inexpensive fabric to test the drape, fit and assembly of the garment. This includes made-to-measure items such as a suit or a wedding dress and haute couture, made by fashion **houses**. This production method incurs very high-level skills in design and manufacture; high-cost materials and high labour costs.

## Toiles or prototypes

Designers create their initial designs either by using muslin, which drapes well for flowing designs or by using linen, canvas or calico for more structured items such as tailored garments. These sample garments are called toiles. The toile can be worked on, marked and adjusted to fit a particular consumer's measurements until the designer and his team are all satisfied. The final toile is an accurate interpretation of the line or cut right down to the button placement or hemline that the designer is seeking. One seamstress or tailor will work on the garment from start to finish. When a collection is created it is common for the toiles to be shown at a 'line-up'. This way the balance of the whole range can be assessed before expensive fabrics are cut to shape! The one-off production method used for a toile or prototype is vital to the success of the final garment.

## Quality counts

Couture clothes are the ultimate in luxury. They require creative designers and workers with the highest expertise in textiles. They have the choice of the most opulent fabrics and the most lavish embellishments; delicate embroidery silks, mother of pearl buttons, bird of paradise feathers, glittering glass beads, usually by the thousand and always hand sewn. If a couture designer wants something for their collection then even if it means finding a supplier from the other side of the world, they will use it. Leading **milliners**, jewellers and shoe designers are brought in to complete the ensemble which may take weeks or months to complete. Haute couture is the most costly and the least cost-effective area of the clothing industry.

Couture survives, despite the outrageous price tags, because the elaborate designs of the famous catwalks eventually end up as ready-to-wear collections and then high street fashions. They also survive thanks to their money-spinning off-shoots such as perfumes, handbags and other accessories.

## Couture today

Contemporary couture designers include Alexander McQueen, John Galliano, Karl Lagerfeld, Emanuel Ungaro, Jean Paul Gaultier and Christian Lacroix. Some will also have ready-to-wear collections while others are exclusively couture.

# Textiles to treasure as a 'one-off'

In the past, the role of handmade cloth and garments was more prominent, more personal and more a part of everyday life than it is today. Textiles embodied the social values and customs of their times, opulent laces and richly woven fabrics displayed wealth and prestige. Fabrics of intricate detail and symbolic design were produced for special occasions and celebrations while richly woven hand embroidered textiles were used for household adornment.

Skilled craftspeople coming from diverse social and financial circumstances created textiles that were a valued and essential part of everyday life. From detailed colourful batiks and costumes embellished with gold thread, to hand-painted and dyed lenghts of cloth and intricately woven wall and bed coverings. All bearing the imprint of their makers' imagination and skill.

Fabulous textiles and fabrics are still created by craftspeople today where they are often treasured as 'one-off' items of art. The work of Ingrid Wagner touches upon the wonder of textiles in the role of 'one-off' production in society today.

Ingrid Wagner is a rug designer who works near St. Peter's Basin in Newcastle. She is a designer who uses bold colour and is inspired by a myriad of cultures and places she has visited. Ingrid has travelled to Georgia to study felt-making and to Morocco to study the weaving and culture of North African rugs! Her studio is stacked full of exotic-looking rugs, vibrant wall hangings and paintings which tell stories about her travels abroad and her particular love of Morocco.

Each piece of Ingrid's work has been designed to commission and is developed from a particular story. She makes her rugs using an air compressed gun tufting method. This cuts and loops the natural fibres she uses. The tufting gun is like drawing with fibre it can move in any direction and uses any colour, thickness or length of wool.

Ingrid uses the gun tufting method of working for all her rugs and wall hangings as it makes construction quicker. Her finished pieces are backed with hessian with a neat strip at the border. Some of her rugs are sheared to produce a smooth velvet-like finish. She uses irregular edges and bold designs to create unique and beautiful textiles.

Such textiles are more like works of art than functional items. Each piece is unique and specially created by the designer.

## Innovative 'one-off' textile production in industry

Usually, 'one-off' textiles and commisioned pieces are created by individual textile artists, but industry also has a role to play in the development of textiles to treasure. This might be in the production of a new fibre or the making of a complete item.

Commercial mills often lack the flexibility to produce unique items as this requires switching equipment from commercial production runs to one-off samples or special runs. Prototype production can also disrupt long commercial runs, adding to the expense of **product development**.

Textiles can be beautiful pieces of art such as these.

However, CSIRO, the Commonwealth Scientific and Industrial Research Organisation, has been helping to address this. Based in Australia, CSIRO provides research and development, consulting, testing and processing services to the wool, cotton, advanced materials and technical textiles industries. It has helped to fund a pilot-scale textile mill which does have the flexibility to produce one-off samples or to do specialist runs at any time.

One of the new technologies it is developing is the 'CCI sample weaving loom'. This loom can rapidly produce small samples, with less wastage of precious yarns. What currently takes 20kg to 40kg of **yarn** on a conventional loom now takes around 0.5kg to produce on the CCI weaving loom.

The loom is customized so it can work with delicate or custom-made fibres not generally made for weaving. For example, the silver-coated copper wire manufactured for the internal mechanisms of watches can now be used to make electronic textiles. This loom can weave threads like this because the CCI is specially adapted to handle delicate and often brittle fibres.

The CSIRO mill has also installed new knitting and weaving machines to develop new materials for emerging and high-tech industries. This will help retail and design specialists to produce small size samples quickly and at minimum expense.

# Designer labels

Designer labels are clothes that have the status of being associated with a designer's name. The designer may not have designed the garment personally – it may have been created by someone from their design team – but it still carries the

designer label. Some consumers prefer to look for specific designer clothes not just because they want to be seen wearing a particular label, but because the clothes are a good fit or they particularly like the cut. Designerwear can be relatively expensive because you are paying for the name as well as the garment. Examples include French Connection, Nicole Farhi and Christa Davies.

These are a few of the shops that sell designer labels.

## Patents

If a designer has created a garment using a new process or has incorporated a totally new idea into the design, they can apply for a **patent**. This prevents another company or person from copying the design for a specified length of time. A patent will only be granted if the product is genuinely original. If necessary, an international patent can be obtained so the product cannot be copied abroad. In textiles, products most likely to require a patent include new fibres, new machinery and equipment used during the processing of fibres and fabrics.

## Second to none

Today it is possible to buy perfectly legitimate designer labels but without paying top prices. Buying from secondhand shops has not only become acceptable, it is also a trendy way to buy your clothes. It is environmentally sound as well because clothes are being 'recycled' rather than thrown away. Often you are supporting a worthwhile charitable cause, too. As an added bonus, when you buy from a secondhand shop, it is unlikely you will see anyone else wearing the same outfit as you! The trend towards buying from secondhand stores is probably also linked to a more relaxed attitude to fashion. Mixing and matching clothes from different eras is all part of the versatile mix of styles characteristic of today's fashion.

Some secondhand stores actually specialize in designerwear. There are plenty of people who will discard their designer jacket because it was from the previous season and there are many more people happy to wear it if it can be bought at a reasonable price.

# Designer jeans

It is thought that the first designer's name to appear on a pair of jeans was that of Gloria Vanderbilt. At a time when many designers still regarded denim jeans as workwear rather than items of fashion, the president of an American manufacturing company, Warren Hirsh, had the idea of producing designer label clothes for the **mass market**. He decided to start with jeans and, as he had a team of professional designers, all he needed was someone to put their famous name to the denims. Eventually he found Gloria Vanderbilt, an heiress who had begun selling her own line of home furnishings. Her signature appeared above a picture of a swan on the back hip pocket of the jeans.

As Warren Hirsh had experience in marketing he decided it would be a good idea for Gloria Vanderbilt to model and advertise the jeans herself. He was hoping they would then appeal to more mature, **suburban** women and he was right because very soon, well-dressed women everywhere were wearing Vanderbilt jeans.

Gloria Vanderbilt jeans are thought to be the first items of designer label clothes produced for the mass market.

# The ecommerce influence

The introduction of new technologies and a new era in consumer shopping has allowed the 'designer label' to keep its status within the market place. Dave Lomax (Bagga Menswear) has capitalized on this consumer trend to develop his designer fashion business changing from a high street premier shop into a web business. This new style of shopping is much more profitable than store generated sales due to the lower overheads of running the business as a website. Like his high street shop, the website sells around 500 lines and specializes in clothing and footwear from Armani, Diesel and G-Star. This system has also enhanced the marketing of 'Bagga' wear through pay-per-click (PPC) advertising, which is a very effective medium. This produces a high volume of sales at a relatively low cost. The biggest bonus however is that ecommerce makes the 'designer label' more competitive on the high street today.

# The cost of clothes

Anyone involved in making and selling clothes is also in the business of making money. Profits are important so money can be ploughed back to improve and expand the business. Profits make for a secure business and give security to the workers. Whether or not a profit is achieved is largely dependent on whether or not consumers buy the garments on offer. However, long before clothes go on sale, careful costings must be worked out to ensure the price is acceptable for both the consumer and the manufacturer.

## Counting the cost

The costing of a garment is usually prepared by a manufacturer's finance department. Once prepared, the costing sheet will be presented to the management for approval. The cost of a new garment must be looked at in relation to all other costs. If an item of clothing is predicted to be in high demand but the production costs are very expensive, it may not be possible to produce it. The ultimate decision will be taken by the management.

The finance department gather their information about costing from a variety of sources. The cutting room or marker planning area will provide details about the amount and type of fabric and any trimmings needed. The purchasing department will know how much the fabric and trimmings cost. The production area will be able to supply information such as the time and costs involved in cutting, sewing and finishing the garment. The more components in a garment and the more operations required during production, the more it will cost to make. The number of

Long before clothes go on sale, costings must be calculated. The price of a garment must be acceptable to both the consumer and the manufacturer.

workers involved and the amount of different machines needed will also affect the cost.

## Costing sheet

Once the finance department have all the necessary information, they can start to complete a costing sheet. This will show details of the costings for:
- materials
- labour
- overheads
- other expenses, including value-added tax (VAT).

Overheads are the additional costs involved in making the garments. Fixed overheads are the costs that have to be paid and will not vary according to type of product being made. These would include, for example, rent of buildings, rates payable to the local authority and insurance of property and equipment. Variable overheads are those that depend on the amount and type of garments being produced. They might include energy, administration costs and maintenance costs. The finance department must work out all the overheads when they prepare a costing sheet.

## The price is right

When all costs are added together, the result is the total cost price of the garment. This is used to decide whether it can be sold at a profit. In other words, whether the price consumers are willing to pay is greater than the total cost of making the garment. Costing sheets are used to determine the selling price and the profit for the company. The amount of profit added can be anything from 10 percent to 100 percent, depending on the type of clothing.

## Price brackets

Many large retailers use a system of **price bracketing**. This means items of clothing are categorized and given a price range. The retailer will only buy manufacturer's products that fit into their price brackets. For example, a retailer may use the following price brackets for female knitwear:

- Bargain £8 – £12
- Cheap £15 – £20
- Average £21 – £35
- Expensive £40 – £60
- Luxury £65 – £80

A manufacturer will know that the retailer's product buyer will only choose goods that fit into their price brackets. This means they must cost their garments very carefully. The amount of profit added will depend on the amount of risk involved in the sale. A **fad** fashion is a high-risk item because consumers are likely to want it for only a short time. Consequently, the price bracket of a fad fashion will be wider than that of a 'safe' garment that the manufacturer knows will sell well.

The female knitwear shown here might fall into a wide price bracket because it is regarded as a fad fashion item.

# Computers and clothes

## CAD/CAM in industry

Computers can be used from the very beginning of the design stage through manufacturing and marketing, to the sale of garments. Computer-aided design (CAD) has enabled designers to produce exciting new fabrics easily and efficiently.

## CAM

Computer-aided manufacture (CAM) is also an important feature of the clothing industry. CAM is a process of making a product using equipment that is controlled by a computer.

## Pattern design

Traditionally all patterns were produced by manipulating cloth around a stand or model of a human shape. The result enabled pattern pieces to be cut, and from these garments could be made. From this developed the idea of basic pattern blocks which (in theory) could

be used to create any style. Today, patterns can be created instantly by computer using a pattern design system (PDS). With both stored information and data that is input by the operator, the system can produce pattern pieces that automatically feature pleats, darts, fullness and seam allowances.

## Grading and marking

Grading and marking systems (GMS) are advanced systems that carry out grading and marker planning. Grading is the process of increasing or decreasing a pattern to produce the same outfit but in a variety of standard sizes. Measurements are fed into the computer, the new sizes are calculated and the altered pattern pieces are produced. Marker planning is the process of accurately marking the patterns so they will match when they are joined together. Features such as zips and buttons are also included.

**Advantages of CAD**

- More complex and creative designs and products can be produced.
- Designers can apply sophisticated techniques to reproduce computerized effects on to fabric.
- More cost and time effective.
- CAD can be effectively combined with freehand drawing.
- It is quicker to manufacture design ideas and makes certain processes less tedious eg. Colour schemes can be altered at the click of a button.
- Information can be collected, stored and transported electronically.

**Advantages of CAM**

- Products can be made to a very high standard.
- More complex products can be manufactured.
- Accurate prototypes or toiles for textile products can be produced.
- It is quicker to manufacture products saving both time and money.
- Controlling the manufacture of items using output devices is more precise, i.e. a die cutter to stamp out pattern pieces.

## Lay planning

A lay plan is an arrangement of pattern pieces that ensures the most economic use of fabric. A light pen is used to move the pattern pieces on the screen so waste is kept to a minimum. This information is stored and can be printed if a small-scale plan of the layout is needed.

## Cutting

In mass or batch production several layers of fabric are cut at the same time to speed up the process. However, a cutting marker may be required if the fabric is to be cut using a cutting tool. This is a sheet with all the pieces marked on it, that guides the cutting tool. A computerized system can produce the cutting marker. However, fully automated cutting systems will cut layers of fabric accurately and consistently using sharp, vertical knives and with little operator intervention.

Pattern pieces can be manipulated on screen to ensure maximum use of the fabric.

## Computer control

CAM enables one person to control an entire range of manufacturing operations with a computer, so it reduces the number of staff a company needs. Also, by allowing computers to control the manufacturing process, tasks are performed in exactly the same way every time, so the risk of human error is reduced.

## PDP

The Product Development Partnership (PDP) consists of a group of suppliers and technology companies who have got together to improve communication in the clothing industry. As more and more companies become computerized, it is clear that different systems need to be compatible for communication purposes. For example, a stock control system may be incompatible with the supplier's ordering system. PDP aims to include the whole supply chain in a compatible system, from fabric production right through to the consumer.

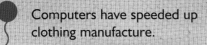
Computers have speeded up clothing manufacture.

# Production systems

Like most areas of manufacturing, the clothing industry relies heavily on production systems. These systems involve a series of activities or parts that:

- are essential to the production
- are connected in an organized way
- cause a change during the production.

A production system may be thought of as a series of interconnections between materials, tasks, machines and components.

## Inputs and outputs

In order for a system to exist, even in a simple form, it requires **inputs**, outputs and processes. The input is everything that is put into the system, so this will include all the materials, the workers, equipment, energy etc. The output is the end-product of the system, so this may be a T-shirt, some fabric or skeins (large bundles) of dyed yarn, depending on the specific system. Clearly something must happen to the inputs in order to achieve the outputs. Anything that affects or changes the inputs is referred to as a process. A system is used to ensure outputs are produced as efficiently as possible.

## Setting standards

As well as ensuring production efficiency, a system can help to maintain standards within the production process. By using a system, a task may be made easier to do or a process may become more efficient. The pace of certain processes can be adjusted when necessary and tasks can be monitored to ensure consistency. Production can be made more cost effective when using a system.

## Defining the boundaries

A system may be a combination of several smaller systems known as sub-systems. The sub-systems rely on one another for the successful production of an output, so if one sub-system breaks down, the overall system will be affected. For this reason it is necessary to define the system boundary or boundaries. Everything belonging to a particular boundary is part of that system. So, a boundary may be established around a particular area of production, perhaps cutting out or finishing. Then, when a system needs to be tested or adjusted, only the processes belonging to that specific system boundary will need to be analyzed.

These items may be regarded as inputs into a system.

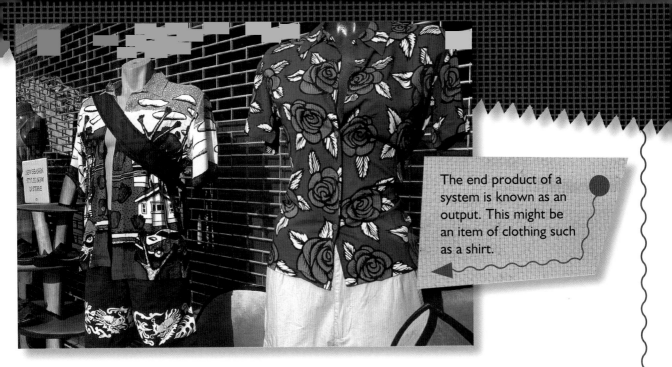

The end product of a system is known as an output. This might be an item of clothing such as a shirt.

# System control

It has already been said that systems can make production more efficient but efficiency really comes into its own when the system is controlled. Today computers are commonly used to control systems in the clothing industry. Computer-aided design (CAD) and computer-aided manufacture (CAM) are the main methods of controlling the design and manufacturing stages (see pages 24–25).

# Feedback

The success of a system is determined by its ability to transform its inputs into outputs. In addition to control, a system relies on feedback to ensure quality outputs are produced. Feedback is the information that is passed back along the system. If it detects a problem, changes to the system can be made straight away. There are two main types of feedback system: open feedback and closed-loop feedback.

## Open feedback

A system of open feedback is used when an adjustment can be made manually during the production. If a computer detects shirts are not being sealed in their packaging correctly then this will show up on a screen. The machine operator can then make the necessary adjustments and production will not be greatly interrupted.

## Closed-loop feedback

A closed-loop feedback system is one where an adjustment is made automatically. Sensors are often used to monitor and alter levels in a system. For example, a sensor can be used to detect temperatures and cause them to increase or decrease as necessary.

# Just-in-time

Special systems are used to monitor stock in many areas of manufacture. In the clothing industry, the system of just-in-time means that stock such as fabric is only ordered when it is needed. The theory behind this is that if expensive stock is kept for long periods it is not actually making any money. On the other hand, it is necessary to have some items in stock all the time if they are likely to be needed. This stock system is known as just-in-case.

# Textiles testing

The clothing industry, as with other textile industries, must assess its products to ensure they meet the needs of the consumers for whom they were designed. Every clothing manufacturer needs to be confident that a successful product is being placed on the market. The assessment may involve scientific testing for garments such as waterproof, weatherproof jackets for mountaineers, or a more aesthetic judgement about some luxury clothes. The process of assessing items is carried out using various evaluation methods and may take place at any stage of design and production.

## Types of evaluation

If garments are tested throughout the whole process, from design to end-product, they are being continuously evaluated. On the other hand, specific aspects may be chosen for selective evaluation – for example, testing the strength of a fastener. If garments are to be tested at the end of the process then the evaluation will be a comprehensive one, covering the whole product. However, whatever type of evaluation is used, there must be standards against which each aspect can be judged. These standards are known as **criteria**.

Some examples of criteria used when evaluating clothes are shown in the box to the right. The criteria for a scientific test may involve a particular set of results so it is easy to assess if the product has met the criteria. A comprehensive evaluation of a garment may be more difficult to assess against criteria because there may be conflicts in the results. If some criteria are met but others are not, a decision is made about which are most important for that particular item.

## Examples of evaluation criteria

- Aesthetics – do consumers find it aesthetically pleasing?
- Cost to the environment – what will the effects be on the environment?
- Fitness for purpose – are all components able to carry out the garment's function?
- Function – does the garment perform the task it is supposed to?
- Safety – does it meet legal safety standards?
- Size – does the garment fit the consumer or meet the standard sizing?
- Special needs – do any special considerations (such as use by the disabled) need to be made?
- Value for money – can it be sold at a price consumers are prepared to pay?

# Product specifications

To ensure a garment meets the needs of its consumer target group, all the criteria used to evaluate it are set out in its product specification. This is written during a design process, after the garment design has been thoroughly researched and tested. The fabrics and components will be specified, as well as the manufacturing processes, constraints of cost, size and time. Clearly, to evaluate a product effectively, it must be assessed against these specifications when it is completed. For example, if the production costs were actually higher than stated in the specification (perhaps due to the manufacturer being let down by a supplier) then the garment may fail to meet the cost criteria. This may then lead to the **target consumer group** being unwilling to pay the higher price necessary to cover the extra costs. The garment has then failed to meet two of its evaluation criteria, when checked against its product specification.

# Tolerance levels

When evaluating some products it is difficult to assess them with 100 percent accuracy. This may be because the production is very complex or the item itself is very complex. For this reason, the clothing industry regularly uses **tolerance levels** when testing certain criteria. This means that the assessment can fall within a previously set range, with an upper and a lower limit. For example, men's trousers may be labelled with a length of 112cm but during the testing procedure the trousers will be acceptable if their length falls within the range 110cm–114cm. Any measurement outside these tolerance levels would make the garment unacceptable. A tolerance level is an example of a constraint placed on a design. A constraint is something that sets limitation, either within a range, like a tolerance level, or something that is precise, like a fabric being waterproof.

# Evaluating textiles

## Market research

A lot of clothes are highly functional while others may be practical but also have an aesthetic appeal. Functional clothes will require scientific testing but most clothes also need to be assessed by the target consumer group. This may be carried out using market research.

Marketing is used to find out what demand there is for particular products and to work out how to encourage the consumer to buy them. Market research can be carried out in many different ways. Here are a few suggestions:

- Interview your target group
- Collect information from magazines, catalogues, leaflets, the internet and TV
- Visit retail outlets and exhibitions
- Use questionnaires and surveys
- Visit local textile manufacturers or find information from CD-Roms and books
- Take photographs or use digital imagery to show the construction of existing products.

To assess whether garments meet consumer needs the market research often involves asking consumers to look at the clothes and answer questions about them. This type of research is more **subjective** because the consumer is giving a personal opinion about something. To make this information easier to assess, there may be a variety of options the consumer can choose from. The research may be in the form of a questionnaire or it could be an interview. Consumers may be on their own or part of a group. The more people included in market research, the more reliable the results are likely to be when collated and analyzed.

Market research plays an important role in finding out what consumers think about products.

## Comparing clothes

In the early stages of a design process, similar existing products are often compared and even **disassembled** in order to develop design ideas. The aim is to produce ideas that will be an improvement on existing products.

However, even when a garment has been completed it may be useful to evaluate it against other similar garments. Comparing items is a useful exercise in market research because consumers can say what they think of a new garment when it is compared with something similar, but perhaps made using a different fabric. Garments may also be compared with or contrasted to clothes that are more expensive, to see whether the consumers are getting more value for money.

# Testing garments

Scientific testing has to be carried out on many items of clothing. Functional clothes such as protective uniforms must pass stringent tests laid down by law. Finished garments will be tested at regular intervals to ensure standards are being maintained. Although this type of testing will mean the product is destroyed in the process, it is an essential part of the evaluation process.

Before a garment is launched on the market, it may go through a trial period. Either a prototype or the final product is worn and used for a period of time to evaluate its success. The trial may involve something as simple as giving a group of parents dungarees for their toddlers for a period of three weeks. During that time the parents have to assess the suitability of the clothes. This may include an evaluation of:

- the fastenings used
- getting the dungarees on and off
- the child's comfort and freedom of movement
- washing and drying the dungarees.

This sort of trialling is particularly useful for clothes that need to be practical, such as uniforms and work clothes. Someone trialling the outfit can say whether the pockets are in the right place and whether they are large enough to hold all the necessary tools and equipment. It must be remembered, though, that it is impossible to please everyone all the time, so the more people involved in the trialling, the easier the results will be to analyze.

# Reviewing the system

Even when a product has been made and the outcome is successful, it is good working practice for a review to take place. This can involve reviewing all stages in the design and manufacturing process. It may be that a manufacturing technique has been used for the first time and, even though it may have worked well during the production of a prototype, there are aspects that can be refined and improved. Equally, the process may work so well that its review will enable the manufacturer to use it in other production areas.

Trialling clothes in a real life situation is important to ensure they are designed and made to meet consumer needs.

# Textile quality

## Consumer quality

The term 'quality' can be defined as a level of excellence. But what may be regarded as excellent by one consumer may not be considered excellent by another. Consumers are likely to judge the quality of clothes in a number of ways, depending on the item. Football shorts, for example, must be hard-wearing, fit properly and be reasonably priced. However, an outfit for a special occasion may be judged on its aesthetic qualities, or what it looks like, rather than its performance. Consumers may also place importance on value for money or price, depending on the garment and what they can afford.

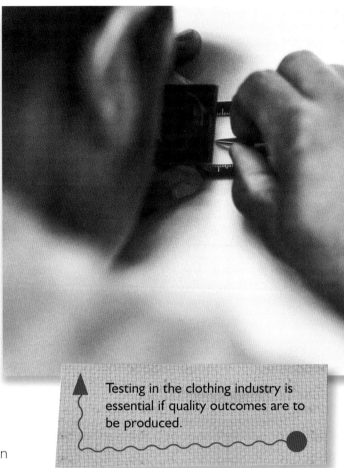

Testing in the clothing industry is essential if quality outcomes are to be produced.

## Industrial quality

The clothing industry also defines quality in terms of levels of excellence. However, their judgements must be based on **objective** measurements rather than subjective ones. Testing is necessary in order to ensure quality outcomes are produced. A company needs a good reputation and loyalty from its consumers and it can only achieve this if it is producing products of a consistently high standard.

Quality has to be assessed throughout the entire process, not just at the end of production, and the product specification must be taken into account. Quality of design and quality of manufacture are separate aspects but they are dependent on one another in the production of a quality item of clothing. Quality is assessed using quality assurance, quality control and attribute analysis.

## Quality assurance

Quality assurance is an overall approach to quality. It ensures standards are maintained as checks are made at every stage, from design to packaging. This gives the consumer the satisfaction of knowing that the company is giving its assurance that standards have been met. Quality assurance relies on everyone in the production process achieving the targets set for their area of work. By giving all workers responsibility in this way, they are more likely to take pride in what they do and that helps the business to run more efficiently. This system is known as Total Quality Management.

## Quality control

Most companies have one or more quality controllers who are in charge of quality control. This is a method of ensuring and maintaining quality at every stage of production. It includes checking the raw materials and components, all steps of production and the final outcome. The quality controller checks that the product is within its tolerance level. However, quality control is not just a system of checks. It is also about ensuring everyone involved knows exactly what to do and how to do it. Instructions for workers must be clear and training given if necessary.

Quality control checks ensure that the product specification is being met. It may include details such as the size of stitches or the type of button. If these do not match the specification, the garment has to be rejected or altered which leads to a loss of time and money.

## Attribute analysis

Another method of ensuring quality products are produced is known as attribute analysis. This involves checking products to see whether or not they have any defects. During the manufacture visual checks are made to see that garments have been assembled in the right way and that the stitching is correct. When attribute analysis is used in mass production, the quality can be assessed mathematically by working out the percentage of faulty goods produced. The smaller the percentage, the better the quality of production.

## Quality signs

It is important for both consumers and the clothing industry that products are labelled to show the standard of the goods. Various quality signs used on textile items are shown here, although there are others that are used on garments. For example, flame retardant clothing can display the quality sign mark CEN if the fabric has fire retardant properties that meet European Union specifications.

The British Standards Institute (BSI) provides 'rules, guidelines and characteristics' to be used in designing and making products. Many British standards have now merged with European standards e.g., the British Standard for Toys is known as BSEN71 which merges the British (BS) with the European (EN) standard. The International Organisation for Standardization (ISO) promotes the development of standardization in designing and making.

Examples of quality symbols that can be found on textile items.

# Consumer protection

Even with rigorous procedures of quality testing in place, it is possible that faulty garments may reach the consumer. In order to protect the consumer against unscrupulous manufacturers who could otherwise get away with selling substandard goods, a number of acts of law have been established.

## Consumer Protection Act 1987

This act of law makes it an offence for anyone to put misleading prices on their goods. For example, if a rail of jumpers states '£19.99 or below' and a consumer chooses a jumper and is charged £25.99, then the sign has been misleading. In this case the consumer has the right to complain. This act also covers sales and special offers.

## Consumer Credit Act 1974

This act provides protection for consumers who purchase goods using credit. It is aimed at credit companies rather than retailers or manufacturers.

## Sale of Goods Act 1979

This act is designed to protect a consumer if faulty goods are purchased, but it also helps to prevent poor quality goods being sold in the first place. The act says:

- Goods must be of merchantable quality, e.g. if a pair of boots are worn once and the heel falls off, they cannot be regarded as good quality.
- Goods must be as described, e.g. a jacket described as 'leather' must not actually be made from a manufactured fabric.

- Goods must be fit for the purpose for which they are to be used, e.g. if a raincoat states 'waterproof' then it must not let in rain.

## Trade Descriptions Act 1968

This act makes it an offence to describe goods (or services) incorrectly. For example, if a garment's care label states it can be washed at 60°C, and the garment shrinks when it is washed at that temperature, the consumer can take it back to the retailer. This act also applies to spoken descriptions so retailers must take care to answer consumers' questions correctly.

## Consumer organizations

There are now a number of organizations whose role it is to help protect consumers. These organizations include:

- Citizens' Advice Bureaux (CAB)
- Office of Fair Trading (OFT)
- **British Standards Institute** (BSI)
- Consumers Association (CA), (publishers of *Which?* magazine)
- Local Authority Trading Standards Officer and Consumer Protection Departments.

In addition, consumers can get a great deal of help from the media. Television programmes such as *Watchdog* and *You and Yours* on the radio publicize information about faulty goods or poor service received by consumers.

## Care labels

Nearly all garments carry care labels giving information about their fibre content, cleaning instructions and any other relevant information. If a label cannot actually be attached to the clothing, on socks for example, it is likely to be provided on the packaging. Examples of some care labels and the details they carry are shown here.

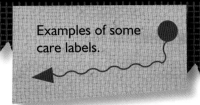

Examples of some care labels.

70% VISCOSE   30% VLAS LIN FLACHS

LINING
VOERING
DOUBLURE          100% VISCOSE
FUTTER

**DRY CLEAN ONLY**

STYLE No. **7 2 9 1 0 0 4**

HAND WASH SEPARATELY
LAVAR SEPARADAMENTE
N.I.F. IMPORTADOR
A.0061711-H
BURTON GROUP PLC
9972

## HLCC

In order to ensure all manufacturers use the same criteria when applying care labels to their textile items, the Home Laundering and Consultative Council has developed an International Textile Care Labelling Scheme. The scheme involves a set of symbols or codes to cover all aspects of laundering textile products. It is called the International Care Labelling Code and examples of its symbols and what they mean are shown on the right.

## Safety labels

As well as having care labels, many items of clothing must be labelled by law to give the consumer information about any risks from fire. Flammability warnings must appear on nightwear and they may include expressions such as 'Carelessness causes fire', 'Warning. Keep away from fire' or 'Low flammability'. The British Standards Institute have set various standards of flammability which are recognized by a BS number. These may be quoted on a label like this, 'Low flammability to BS 5722'.

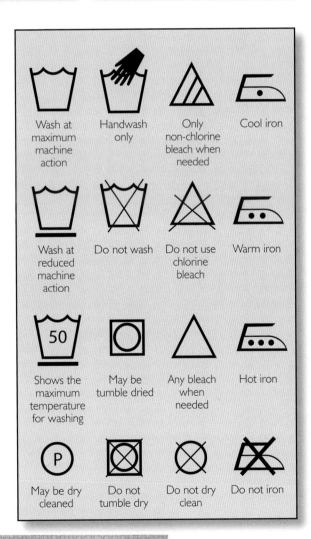

Wash at maximum machine action | Handwash only | Only non-chlorine bleach when needed | Cool iron

Wash at reduced machine action | Do not wash | Do not use chlorine bleach | Warm iron

Shows the maximum temperature for washing | May be tumble dried | Any bleach when needed | Hot iron

May be dry cleaned | Do not tumble dry | Do not dry clean | Do not iron

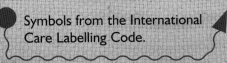

Symbols from the International Care Labelling Code.

# The jeans success story

## Levi Strauss & Co.

Levi Strauss are one of the world's largest brandname clothing companies. They manufacture and market jeans and casual sportswear using the following brand names; Levis®, Dockers® and Slates®. The Levis company has registered the Levis® trademark in more than 200 countries.

Levis Strauss & Co. employ approximately 1600 staff at their San Francisco headquarters, in the United States, and another 30,000 people worldwide. They have 32 production facilities and 29 customer service centres throughout the world.

## Levi history

Levi Strauss was a Bavarian immigrant who went to San Francisco in 1853. When he first arrived he was told he would need some hardwearing trousers, so he made some for himself out of canvas. This could be said to be the first pair of Levi jeans! Over the next twenty years he built up a very successful business selling dry goods and manufacturing work clothes which included 'waist overalls' that we know today as jeans.

When miners began to complain of torn pockets caused by the heavy gold nuggets they carried, Levi Strauss decided to develop a method of reinforcing the pockets. He enlisted the help of a tailor called Jacob W. Davis who came up with the idea of using a copper wire to rivet the pockets. The rivet was patented in 1873 and this was the start of the rivets so familiar on today's jeans.

When Levis Strauss died in 1902 he left his thriving business to his four nephews. The family continue to control it today.

## Levi's® 501®

Levi's® 501® jeans were first created in the 1800s and were given the number 501 around 1890. They are distinguished by their button-fly and their Shrink-To-Fit® nature. They are the oldest and best selling product of Levi Strauss & Co. They are made from serge de Nimes denim, a type of cotton twill originally made in Nimes, France, over 500 years ago. The denim is dyed blue with indigo (see opposite). In 1936 the Red Tab Device® was created to help identify Levi's® 501® jeans from a distance. These jeans were called waist overalls up until 1960.

Today Levi's® 501® jeans are made in approximately 108 sizes with 20 different finishes and fabrics. The typical production for one pair requires 1.6 metres (1 ¾ yards) of denim and 195 metres (213 yards) of thread.

The ever-popular Levi jeans.

## Indigo blue

Traditionally the woad plant (Isatis tinctoria) produces the blue colour called indigo that is used to dye denim, although a synthetic version was developed in the late 1800s. Recently the Ministry of Agriculture and several companies have funded a research project into the development of a new crop of woad to produce natural indigo. Gorham & Batesman (Agriculture) Ltd., based in Norfolk, are one of the Woad Project partners. They have been trialling the pilot crop, which can produce blue dye in just twelve minutes. India and China supply most of the natural dye to Britain but growing consumer demand for natural processes and sources should mean that the project will be profitable.

In addition it has five buttons and five rivets. Thirty-seven separate sewing operations are involved in the making of a single pair of Levi's® 501® jeans.

## Cutting and stitching

A roll of denim cloth is referred to as a bolt and each one weighs about a quarter of a tonne. The cloth is cut using an electric saw which slices through 120 layers at one time. One bolt of denim can be used to cut about 60 pairs of jeans.

Jeans are well known for their double row of stitching on the back pockets and inside legs. Today this double stitching is called Arcuate Design® and it is one of the oldest trademarks used in clothing manufacture. It was first used in 1873 and was so popular that during the Second World War, stitches were painted on back pockets because rationing meant thread was in short supply.

## Rivets

In the early days of jeans making, rivets were placed on both front and back pockets. As the wearing of jeans became more widespread in America there were complaints that the rivets on the back pockets were scratching school chairs and horses' saddles. In 1937 this problem was initially solved by covering the rear rivets. However, since 1967 back pocket rivets have been replaced altogether with reinforced stitching.

# Textile project: denim

For this project, you will be producing a portfolio. A portfolio is a collection of ideas presented together. If you wish to go on and make one or more items from your collection then this will extend your experience of working with textiles. You could develop your own pattern from your sketches or you could use a commercial pattern that may, or may not, need to be adapted.

## Denim range

This project involves creating a new range of denim clothing. The range could be for yourself, or for a particular group of consumers such as toddlers. It could be a particular type of clothing such as sports or casual wear. Another alternative would be to design a range from one item of clothing, for example, a range of shirts, or a new range of jeans. Keep your target consumer group in mind all the time you are designing.

Read through the following information before you start your designs but remember you can sketch rough ideas at any time, whenever you feel inspired.

## Inspired by denim

Jeans provide a famous and lasting example of workwear that has moved into the area of fashion. Following the popularity of jeans as an item of clothing for men, women and children, other textile items have branched into denim. Denim is now regularly used for many types of clothing as well as accessories and household furnishings.

Apart from blue, denim is now available in a range of colours and in different weights or thicknesses. Variations include denim that is faded or patterned, stretch denim and patchwork denim. In addition to jeans, clothes that can be made using denim include shorts, shirts, hats, shoes, dresses and skirts. Denim is a 'universal' fabric suitable for all ages and both genders.

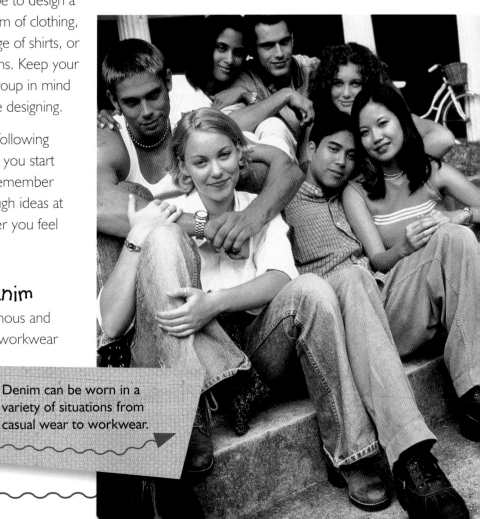

Denim can be worn in a variety of situations from casual wear to workwear.

# Researching the fabric

- The word denim is an Americanisation of the French name "serge de Nimes," a fabric which originated in Nimes, France, during the Middle Ages.

- Authentic blue denim takes its characteristic colour from interweaving indigo (blue) and white threads together.

- Denim's right-hand twill construction means that one colour predominates on the fabric surface.

- Research a fabric thoroughly before starting to produce design ideas. Make sure you record any important research using sketches, notes, swatches of fabric, magazine cuttings, photographs etc.

- Yarns used in denim may vary in weight - jeans with heavier yarns are expected to be slightly more durable.

## Denim

- The way denim is woven makes the fabric very strong and durable.

- Some denims have an extra layer of fabric fused to the inside knee area. The process, which is called vulcanizing, adds reinforcement and durability to the knee area.

- Most jeans are made from 100% cotton or a blend of 50% cotton and 50% polyester. A new fibre - Tencel, has been introduced in denim blends with polyester to enhance its characteristics.

- Italian sailors from Genoa wore cotton trousers and the French call Genoa and the people who live there, "Genes." The name "jeans" was applied to the pants as well.

- Denim fabric can be treated in many different ways. Popular treatments include pre-washed, stone-washed, sandblasted, and vintage/dirty.

# Presenting ideas

Look carefully at your research before starting work on your portfolio. Decide how you wish to present your ideas and what you will show them on. You could use a sketch pad or present them on one large display board perhaps as a mood board. The clothes should be sketched in pencil and then either coloured in or samples of colour created around each labelled drawing. Your sketches can be enhanced with swatches of fabric, fastenings, even notes about construction techniques if you wish.

One way to present your design ideas might be as a 'denim book'. Decorate a piece of A3 card with some denim fabric and fold it in half to form the sleeve of an A4 book.

The clothing designs could be presented on white A4 card with perhaps a corner covered in denim to give a consistent feel throughout. The A4 design sheets can then be slipped inside the denim sleeve. Presentation is very important with fashion design so plan this carefully before you begin.

Clothes can be displayed on their own or on models. If you find it difficult to draw people an outline can be traced so each model is the same every time.

Building a range of portfolios such as this one can help to develop both design and making skills because it is important to understand how garments are made in order to design them successfully.

# finishing techniques

The way clothes are treated by the consumer is largely dependent on the method of their construction and fibre content. A non-woven fabric such as felt will not withstand a machine wash whereas a fabric made from 100 percent cotton will wash well but will also need to be ironed. However, the properties of fabric can be altered or enhanced with the application of special finishing techniques.

Finishing techniques are usually permanent and so will last the lifetime of the garment. However, some clothes have a temporary finish that will be lost after the fabric is cleaned. Other finishes are renewable and can be reapplied, in the same way leather shoes can be sprayed to protect them against the rain.

A waterproof finish is essential for rainwear.

## Physical finishes

These finishes are applied mechanically and result in a change in the fabric's appearance and/or texture. They include calendering, filling, raising and tentering.

- Calendering – produces fabric with a smooth surface and silky lustre. **Chintz** is an example of a plain weave cotton that has been calendered. The process is relatively straightforward as it involves the fabric being passed between heated rollers. The rollers can be engraved to produce a fabric with an embossed pattern. Eventually this finish will wear off.
- Filling – used to make a loosely woven cheap fabric appear smooth and strong by soaking it in a starch solution. The fabric then goes through the calendering process. This finish will only last until the starch is rinsed away in the first wash.

- Raising – an example of a permanent finishing technique. The fabric passes through a series of rollers covered in wire which gently tease out the fibre ends from the weave. The technique must be carried out gently otherwise the fibres would tear and weaken the fabric. The result is a raised surface and a fluffy texture. Such fabrics can be used for winter clothes that help to keep the wearer warm.
- Tentering – applied to fabrics that have lost their shape during the construction process. In order to restore the shape, the fabric is dipped in a chemical bath, then it travels through a machine which grips the **selvedges** with tiny clips. The machine holds the fabric while it is heat dried, and the finished fabric returns to its correct shape. Tentering does not have a permanent effect so the fabric may shrink again once it has been washed.

# Chemical finishes

Unlike physical finishes, a chemical finish can be applied at any point during the production process, from fibre to fabric. Some examples are given here.

- Flameproofing finishes – applied to yarns and fabrics. Items such as soft furnishings and children's nightwear have to be produced according to strict guidelines laid down by the British Standards Institute. Such items must also be clearly labelled because the flammability protection may be lost if they are washed incorrectly.

- Crease-resistant finishes (permanent) – reduce the need for ironing. Fabrics that crease easily, and therefore are likely to be given this treatment, include cotton, linen and viscose. A resin is applied to the fabric which is then dried and heat-set.

- Stain- and dirt-resistant finishes – used on furnishing fabrics and curtains. Sometimes manufacturers provide this as an optional extra when selling sofas, armchairs and sofabeds. The finish works by providing a barrier over the fibres preventing dirt and grease from penetrating the fabric.

- Shrink-resistant finishes – often applied to wool fibres as they are most likely to shrink. The chemicals used prevent the scales on the wool fibres from interlocking which causes **felting** when the wool is washed. The finish may be applied to the fibre or after the item has been fully constructed. It is due to this finish that you now see 'machine washable' labels on wool garments.

## Self-cleaning clothes!

Scientists have been experimenting with an idea to impregnate bacteria into every single fibre of a fabric. The bacteria would live, breed and eat up the dirt, creating self-cleaning clothes. It is hoped that garments may be able to support a variety of bacteria engineered to eat odour-causing chemicals and human sweat. Other bacteria might secrete waterproof and protective coatings to extend the life of clothing and produce antiseptic for bandages.

When a garment is impregnated with a strain of E. coli designed to feed on human sweat and the proteins that cause body odours, wearing it would jolt the bugs into action. For further garment enhancement, different strains of bacteria could be sprayed onto the fabric surface to douse it with additional nutrients. You could end up having to feed your shirt instead of washing it!

- Waterproofing finishes – used on items such as raincoats, jackets, umbrellas and hats. The chemicals involved, usually silicone, prevent water from soaking into the fabric yet still allow air to pass through. However, once the fabric becomes **saturated**, water will soak through it.

# Careers in the clothing industry

This page describes some of the main types of employment within the clothing industry. Like most areas of manufacturing, the employment structure will vary from company to company, and a variety of other jobs are also likely to be available.

## Retail buyer

Clothes are usually sold by retailers. The retailer supplies products according to the consumer demand. It is the responsibility of the retail buyer to anticipate the needs of the market. This rather difficult task involves estimating what consumers are likely to buy and in what quantity. The buyer orders the goods from the manufacturer and decides their price bracket. In a small business, the buying may be carried out by the owner. A large company may employ several buyers who specialize in a particular area such as accessories or children's wear.

## Fashion designer

Today, a designer needs to have knowledge of all aspects of clothing production. This gives him or her the ability to anticipate which styles and construction techniques can be used in mass production. A designer must be able to produce sketches that are drawn to scale. These differ from fashion drawings, where the body is often **elongated**. Designers produce working drawings which contain all the information needed for a pattern to be made. Computer-aided design (CAD) packages are also used by many designers today (see page 24).

## Pattern cutter

Pattern cutters are considered by many to be the most important technicians in the whole process of garment manufacture. They fall into two categories – those that work in the design department to produce prototype paper patterns and those that produce the final production pattern made from card, plastic or metal.

## Textile designer

The emphasis on fibre technology in the clothing industry has increased in recent years, and so has the importance of the textile designer. These designers may work in conjunction with a fashion designer. Together they can anticipate the market, in terms of style and fabric. They are creative people who may have a background in textile science.

A background in textile science is useful for a career in textile design.

# Sample machinist

The sample machinist is responsible for making up a garment and assessing whether it is possible to mass produce it. The amount of time it will take and the costs involved also have to be considered. A sample machinist will be experienced enough to estimate the most logical order for garment assembly. An in-house model will try on the sample garment so it can be adjusted if necessary.

# Cutting room manager

The cutting room is where all fabric cutting takes place. Depending on the size and type of company, different types of machines and numbers of people are employed to do the cutting. The manager of the cutting room has to oversee all processes and is responsible for the quality of the cutting. The manager must also ensure the cut pieces are passed on to the production area at the correct time.

# Assembly machinists

There are many types of assembly systems in use today (see pages 26–27). Technology is becoming more and more advanced, but basically garments may be constructed in two ways. A machinist may be given all the component parts and is responsible for the garments from start to finish. This method is usually used by small companies. Alternatively, garments may be produced using a **production line** assembly where a machinist will be responsible for one aspect of the construction. Special machine operators are trained to finish garments by using **overlockers**, buttonhole and button-sewing machines, multi-needle machines and so on.

# The presser

Another specialized area of garment construction is the pressing of clothes. Some pressing is essential during assembly because it cannot be done properly when the garment is complete. This is usually done using a hand iron. The final finishing press may be done by hand or machine, using specialized steam and vacuum presses, or a mixture of both. Trained operators are required to carry out the pressing.

These jobs listed above may seem to be the obvious choice within the fashion industry however, working in public relations, fashion journalism, prediction and forecasting, photography, as a fashion stylist or in fashion illustration is also just as exciting!

# Resources

## Books

The following books are useful for students studying GCSE Design and Technology:

| | |
|---|---|
| *GCSE Textiles Technology for OCR* | Heinemann |
| Carey Clarkson, Jayne March and Joy Palmer | 2002 |
| (student book and teacher resource file) | |

| | |
|---|---|
| *Revise for OCR GCSE Textiles Technology* | Heinemann |
| Carey Clarkson and Maria James | 2003 |

| | |
|---|---|
| *GCSE Design and Technology for AQA* | Heinemann |
| *Textiles Technology* | 2006 |
| Rose Sinclair and Sue Morgan – student book | |
| Carey Clarkson and Justine Simmons – teacher resource file | |

The following books are useful for more detailed information on the clothing industry:

| | |
|---|---|
| *Fashion design* – second edition | Laurence King Publishing |
| Sue Jenkyn Jones | 2005 |

| | |
|---|---|
| *Clothing Technology* | Europa Lehrmittel |
| Von Eberle | 2004 |

## I.C.T.

www.craftscouncil.org.uk/exhib.htm
*Provides details of forthcoming arts and crafts events throughout the country*

www.levistrauss.com
*To find out more about Levi jeans*

www.textile-toolkit.org.uk
*Includes news, competitions, details of events and a chat forum for students; there is also a CD-ROM available for use as a teaching aid for GCSE textiles*

www.worldtextile.com
*Publishes a variety of textile-related journals*

www.ingridwagner.com
*Information about the art of rug creation and paintings from the world journeys of Ingrid Wagner.*

www.standards.dfes.gov.uk/schemes2/secondary
*Information from The Standards Site: producing batches – textiles*

# Places to visit

Luton Museum and Art Gallery
Wardown Park
Luton LU2 7HA
(Tel no: 01582 546722)
*This museum provides comprehensive information about the hat industry*

# Contacts

The Crafts Council
44a Pentonville Road
London N1 9BY
(Tel no: 020 7278 7700)
*Provides up-to-date information about art and crafts exhibitions and shows; also produces a magazine called Crafts, available on subscription*

Department of Trade and Industry (DTI)
Clothing, textiles and footwear unit.
1, Victoria Street,
London SW1H 0ET
Tel: 020 7215 5000
www.dti.gov.uk

# Other useful contacts

Textiles Magazine
The Textile Institute
International Headquarters
First Floor
St. James Buildings
Oxford Street
Manchester M1 6FQ
www.textileinstitute.org
*Articles and written reports about new innovations within the textile industry, designer information and international news*

# Journals

World Clothing Manufacturer
World Textile Publications Ltd.
Perkin House
1 Longlands Street
Bradford
West Yorkshire BD1 2TP
(Tel no: 01274 378800)
*A magazine written for the clothing industry worldwide*

# Glossary

**bespoke** describes clothes that are custom-made by a tailor

**British Standards Institute** professional organization which decides which tests must be applied to which textile products, and sets the standards for the tests

**chintz** glazed or shiny fabric, often made of cotton and used mainly for furnishings

**client** person or company for whom a designer is producing a design or range of designs

**component** part of a garment prior to assembly including accessories

**couture** short for 'haute couture' (see below)

**criteria** standards of judgement that are used, for example, in evaluating the quality of textile products

**disassemble** take apart a garment or textile item in order to find out more about its construction

**elongate** make something extra long; for example the legs of models in fashion drawings are usually drawn disproportionately long

**fad** a short-lived fashion

**felting** matting effect that occurs when fabric, especially wool, is washed at too high a temperature, or too vigorously

**garment performance** extent to which a garment meets performance standards such as being waterproof or having good stretch recovery

**grading** producing pattern pieces in a range of sizes

**haute couture** French term meaning high-quality clothes, designed and made for a very limited market

**house** the fashion industry's term for 'company'

**input** everything that is put into the production system, including materials, workers, equipment and energy

**labour-intensive** involving a lot of work and taking a lot of time

**marker planning** process of accurately marking the patterns so they will match when they are joined together

**market** consumers, or a particular sector of consumers

**marketing** all activities involved in getting garments to consumers; for example selling, advertising, promoting

**market research** research carried out to find out what consumers think about existing products or about new products, or to find out about their needs

**mass market** consumers, on a large scale

**milliner** a person who makes hats

**mood board** display board covered with pictures, sketches, swatches etc, used to create a mood or feeling about a product to be designed; also known as a 'theme board'

**objective** something that depends on facts rather than a person's point of view

**output**  end-product of manufacture; for example a finished garment

**outside contractor**  company which takes on work for another company, either because it is a specialist task or to help during times of excessive workload

**overlocker**  machine that will simultaneously stitch, trim and neaten seams

**patent**  owning the sole right to a new product or process; it has to be applied for

**perceived consumer need**  result of market research; what researchers believe consumers want

**price bracket**  a price range given to items of clothing that have been categorized

**product development**  process of producing and developing new ideas in order to improve on a product or to create a new one

**production line**  production carried out on a garment or product, one process at a time, by different workers

**product specification**  precise details about a particular product – such as type of fabric and size of stitches, relevant manufacturing processes, constraints of cost, size and time – so that it can be reproduced on a large scale

**promote**  publicize something in order to sell it

**prototype**  model of a design idea, used to test its suitability for production

**saturate**  make completely wet

**selvedges**  firm area of fabric created by strong warp threads (threads running vertically) running along the edges of the fabric

**stock**  all items available for sale by a retailer or manufacturer

**subjective**  something that depends on a person's point of view or opinion rather than on fact

**suburban**  residential area that is on the outskirts of a town or city

**target consumer group**  group of consumers such as the elderly, teenagers, or sportswomen being targeted for a product because they are the ones most likely to buy it

**toile**  garment modelled in calico or similar fabric during prototype stage

**tolerance level**  in evaluating a garment, a set range of acceptability, with an upper and a lower limit, that must be met; for example when the specification on trouser length is 112cm, the tolerance level may be 110cm–114cm

**yarn**  single strand of fibres that have been spun together

# Index